CUMBRAE Since the War

The author at the door of his photographic and fancy goods shop at 9 Guildford Street, 1960.
At present the premises are used as the Hydro board's showroom.

ISBN 1 84033 190 9

The publishers regret that they cannot supply copies of any pictures featured in this book. Instead, enquiries should be addressed to Walter Kerr, photographer, Millport.

The wishing well is steeped in history and folklore. It is written that when St Ninian landed at the north end of Cumbrae he walked round the coast and after passing Balloch Bay stopped and refreshed himself at a spring. It is from this spring that the wishing well's water comes. A little chapel dedicated to the saint was built at the site; more about this can be found in Lytteil's book *Isle of Cumbrae*, as well as in A. T. McConnochie's *Cumbrae Old and New* in the section on the battle of Largs. The water from the well is pure and crystal clear, and at one time an iron cup hung by a chain at the side of the well. To make a wish a pebble from the shore has to be dropped into the bowl into which the water pours before a drink is taken. It is amazing the number of people who still do this, even today, and despite the fact that nothing is written down about the tradition.

INTRODUCTION

Cumbrae is situated in the Firth of Clyde between the Isle of Bute and the North Ayrshire mainland. The road round the coast of the island is called the Outer Circle and measures 10¼ miles. A second road called the Inner Circle leads to the highest point on the island, the Glaidstane, 417 feet above sea level. There is an indicator here and many locations around the Clyde coast can be seen from this spot. The south of Cumbrae is one large bay with five small islands in it, and it is on this coast that the town of Millport is situated, therefore enjoying the sunniest position.

To the east of the town is Kames Bay, which has a gently sloping beach, making it very safe for children; the harbour at the pier is also a favourite place for children to play. Newton Beach, well-known for its donkey and pony rides, is in the centre of Millport. In the last few years a new beach has begun to form in front of the sea wall, while to the west of the pier is Knox's Port, a small cove of sand, the approach to which is over rocks.

The next beach along is the Foulport at West Bay. This did not take its name from decaying seaweed as some people think, but from the name Foulsport, which means Port of the Tall Men, as it was believed that there had once been a settlement of Norsemen here. This small bay is better know today as the Cosy Corner.

The Old Pier at the harbour in Millport is kept in good condition and is used by small cruisers, fishing boats and a number of private yachts and pleasure craft. All commercial and passenger traffic travels by Caledonian MacBrayne car ferries which operate between Largs Pier and Cumbrae Slip at the north-east of the island, where the distance between Cumbrae and the mainland is shortest. During the summer the timetable for ferries is every fifteen minutes and in the winter it is every hour (although extra runs are made as necessary when services are busy). With such easy access the island is a favourite destination for sponsored cycle groups and walkers, as the road round it is reasonably flat. Many individuals and family groups also come as cycles can be hired from one of three cycle hirers.

There are four churches in Millport. The Cathedral of the Isles (Scottish Episcopal), the Parish Church, Our Lady of Perpetual Succour and the Evangelical Church (the latter is not used at present as its congregation is so small). The Cathedral of the Isles is recorded in the *Guinness Book of Records* as being the smallest cathedral (of old foundation) in use in the United Kingdom. The architect was William Butterfield and it was built in 1849–51. Its nave is only 40 x 20 feet.

Cumbrae is a holiday island and is very busy in the summer. Harriers from amateur athletic clubs come for the annual race round the island, and there is also an occasional cycle race, with riders from several different clubs taking part. The local dramatic club present shows every week, and most years a group of young people called the Summer Mission hold services on the beach each morning during July.

The Glasgow holiday weekend at the end of September is a time of carnival celebration in Millport. There is a bonfire, a firework display and shops and houses are decorated. Over 1,000 padella lights flicker on the Eilans in the bay and along the promenade. There is street entertainment and the passenger steamer MV *Balmoral* arrives laden with passengers. Many private yachts and motor boats anchor in the bay, and prizes are awarded for the best decorated flat, shop, hotel, boarding house and boat.

There are five islands in Millport bay. The Leug, the Spoig and the Clach are small rocks which are covered at high tide. The other two are known as the Eilans (Gaelic for islands) and lie opposite Newton Beach, where they provide shelter for boats moored in the bay. On rare occasions at exceptionally low tides it is possible to wade out to the Inner Eilan. The last time this happened was in February 1996. It was about 6 p.m. and when word got around the town about 100 people came to either wade or watch and there was quite a party atmosphere. One young man was able to wade out to the Outer Eilan wearing thigh waders. This island has a green navigation light on it acting as a warning to passing vessels.

Cumbrae has an 18-hole golf course where many visiting clubs come to play. Each year the Cumbrae Cup is played for on the course. The bowling green has three greens and a putting green, and clubs from the mainland come to play here too. There are also three tennis courts and a crazy golf course. Football is popular at the West Bay park and an annual knockout competition for the Finlayson Cup is played with visiting clubs participating throughout the summer. The clay pigeon club holds an annual shoot in September, and again competitors come from Bute and the mainland to participate.

Millport has had a cinema for as long as anyone can remember. After the First World War John Dymock, the local burgh surveyor and sanitary inspector, ran the cinema from the town hall (where it is still located today). In the early days films were silent, but a piano hidden by a curtain at the side of the stage provided incidental music. That was as long as the pianist, Miss Polly Graham, didn't become so engrossed in the film that she forgot to play, in which case Mr Dymock marched down and uttered a few choice words before the music resumed.

In the early 1930s sound projectors were installed and the first talkie shown was *The Blue Danube*. Leslie Lynn organised variety shows on the seafront during the summer and later in a corrugated iron building in College Street. He took over the cinema, which was managed by a local man called Jack Brown. In 1936 I got a job as an usher. At the time Willie Dewhurst was the projectionist and Jack Duncan was the spool boy. There was no electricity on the island then and the cinema had to generate its own using a generator – during the show we had to run down to the large diesel engine below the hall and top it up. Jack Brown later left to become manager at the Odeon cinema in Glasgow. He went on to manage cinemas in Hamilton, Renfrew, Blantyre and Dennistoun while his brother Kenny became manager of the cinema in Millport.

The cinema was open fully from Easter to October but only on Saturdays and Mondays in the winter. At the height of the summer season there was only one show on a Saturday night, after which the hall was cleared of seats which were slid down a chute to be stowed below. The floor was swept, the screen rolled up and dances were held, with music provided by the same band that played at Leslie Lynn's variety show.

When I returned to Millport after the Second World War (during which I had been held as a POW), I began a photographic business and didn't return to the cinema, although my younger brother had worked there for a while during the war. Millport Town Council leased the town hall to Archie McCulloch in 1961 for use as a cinema, and he was in charge until regionalisation. As the projectors were old and causing problems by then, the town council decided to purchase two new ones before handing the reins over to Cunninghame District Council. 16 mm projectors were bought as 35 mm ones were too expensive.

At the same time I was approached and asked to be projectionist. I was eventually persuaded to take the job, which was hard-going at first with shows every night and on wet mornings, plus cartoon shows for the children and late night horror screenings at the weekend (I was running my business and two shops at the same time). Unfortunately new film releases are not now being made in 16 mm and due to the difficulty of getting films last year, the cinema was only open for one night a week over six weeks in the summer.

This book contains a few photographs from my extensive collection of negatives, taken since 1950 during my time as a photographer in Millport. I was born on the island, as were my parents and my grandfather, so I know a little of its history. Despite being only three and three-quarter miles long by two miles wide, the selection of pictures in this book illustrates that much has changed and taken place on Cumbrae in the years since the Second World War.

The mobo broncos were owned by Walter and Effie Kerr (the author and his wife) and were located at the back of the Garrison next to the merry-go-round. Children paid 3d. to ride the broncos to the end of a concrete strip and back – something that they enjoyed very much, although the concrete was very sore on the toys' wheels. These children are under starter's orders in 1958. There was a pedal on each side just like stirrups and to propel the bronco forward the rider had to stand up on the pedals. This made the front legs move forward and lock. Sitting back down on the bronco made the back legs move forward then the whole process was repeated again. I well remember the day when a grandmother arrived with her young grandson. The little boy didn't know how to ride the bronco so grandma, sitting on a seat near the concrete strip, issued instructions in a loud Glasgow accent. 'Stand up and then sit down on your bum and keep doing it!' The youngster became an expert very quickly. The broncos were in use until 1959.

This area at the back of the Garrison was a sun trap where many people sat and enjoyed music, played on a loudspeaker from the children's merry-go-round. At the beginning of the rock and roll era the concrete strip (usually used for the mobo broncos) was cleared between 1 and 2 p.m., rock and roll music was played and teenagers came to dance, a sight that attracted many spectators. The Garrison is situated at the centre of Millport and was built *c.*1745 by Captain James Crawford, a customs officer who was captain of a revenue cutter stationed at Millport. He bought the land it stands on from the Marquis of Bute. In 1819 the Garrison was sold to the 6th Lord Glasgow. For a short time before the Second World War it was used as a hydro, but this closed before war broke out when the building was reopened to house Mearnskirk Hospital, whose staff and patients were evacuated there from Glasgow. The burgh offices were located in the Garrison from 1948 until 1999 when the building was declared unsafe (over the years it also housed a museum, library, gas office, restaurant and snack bar, and studio). In June 2001 it was gutted by fire.

Two youngsters enjoying a ride on the merry-go-round in the Garrison grounds in 1956. At one time there were amusements in what is now known as the DA (Development Association) Hall and the manager of these was Bill Austin. It was he who installed the merry-go-round as a sideline. After the amusements closed Bill left the island and sold the merry-go-round to Effie and Walter Kerr. The DA Hall is used by local community groups with the Boys' Brigade meeting there on Fridays and the local pipe band on Tuesdays. The Women's Rural Institute gather there once a month on Thursday evenings. During the summer the Cumbrae Dramatic Club put on their shows there, and the hall is also used for fund-raising events such as jumble sales.

Children taking part in a bathing beauty competition in 1960. This was one of the events organised by the Development Association, and there were separate competitions for four different age groups, both for girls and boys (their competitions were for best-looking boy). The Development Association was established in the 1950s to provide entertainment for summer visitors, and a student was employed to help organise events. On Saturdays a stall was erected for shooting competitions and in the evenings bingo sessions were held. Tug-o-war competitions between teams from the various public houses were popular, as were the ladies' football matches. These last two events were held at the public park at West Bay.

Glamorous Granny competitions were another of the events that were organised for summer visitors, and this group was photographed in 1960. Like the Miss Millport and children's competitions, these contests were held every fortnight. The Development Association's first president was George Fraser, electrician, followed by John Barr, plumber and Walter Kerr, photographer. When it was wound up in 1987 the last president was Harry Garden, coal merchant and builder.

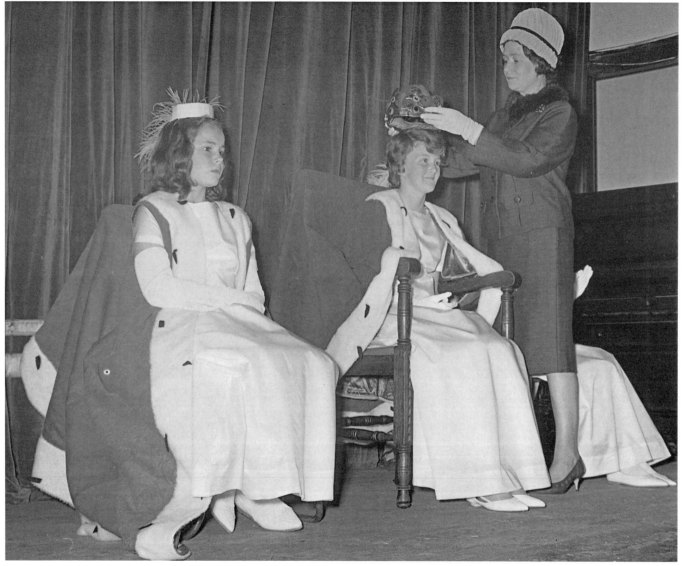

Betty Roberts, wife of Provost Farquhar Roberts, crowning Millport's first Cumbrae Queen, Joan Ferguson, in 1964. Joan's father was the manager of the local co-operative store. Peggy Macrae, wife of the actor Duncan Macrae, was the organiser of the first festival and I was the photographer. Joan, now married, had triplets 22 years ago and lives in Greenock. This crowning ceremony takes place every year and until the present day has only twice had to be held indoors due to bad weather. The very first crowning was one of these occasions!

A fancy dress competition held at the side of the Garrison building in 1987. The local Chinese restaurant decided to enter and very appropriately chose a Chinese dragon. This was a great success and the owner of the restaurant, Peter Shek, can be seen here beating the drum. Fancy dress competitions were held regularly during Harry Garden's presidency of the DA when there was one most Sundays in the summer.

Millport Bowling Club was inaugurated in 1871 with Andrew Speirs as the president. A ladies' section was formed in 1942 and its first president was Mrs C. Melvin. In 2000 the two sections of the club amalgamated with all members paying the same subscription rate, although separate male and female presidents were retained. The club is situated in Bute Terrace and has three greens as well as a putting green. During the summer there are many competitions for local members and visiting clubs. Weather permitting a few ends are played on the second day of every year and in 2002 sixteen players took part playing seven ends.

The outdoor curling pond is situated at the top of the island. During the summer it is drained of water and while still empty at the end of summer club members gather to cut down the weed which has grown and enjoy a barbecue. The pond is then filled in the hope of cold enough weather to freeze it, although due to mild winters in recent years it has not frozen hard since 1995. Despite this there is a flourishing curling club and members go to the mainland to play at indoor rinks. The Dumfries Cup is contested between teams from Millport and Rothesay and must be played for on floating ice. This photograph was taken in 1986.

This local band, the Cumbraeans, was one of the first bands to play at the Cumbrae Club in Howard Street. Featured from left to right in 1969 are Robert Liddle, Ian Weannie, Pat Chalmers and Dennis Kelly. The club was established in the former Territorial Hall by Archie McCulloch, who bought the hall in 1961. It was an upmarket members club, and every Saturday during the summer there were cabaret shows which were so popular that bookings were taken to secure tables. Men had to wear ties and ladies wore their best clothes. Archie invited many of his friends in show business to take part in the cabaret.

His wife, Kathy Kay, who sang with Billy Cotton, was a regular performer. Duncan Macrae appeared quite often, as did Andy Stewart and Glen Dailly. There were dancing girls known as the Cumbrae Kittens with music led by the well-known pianist Douglas Wylie. After Douglas left Ivy Polane became the resident pianist. Archie latterly sold the club to Marie and Dennis Kelly who carried it on very successfully, although on different lines as they did not have the show business contacts. The club changed hands several times afterwards and currently the building it occupied stands empty.

The Millport football team line-up of 1955 photographed in the public park. *Back row* (left to right): Ian Spiers; Bill Spiers; Jack Templeton; Norrie Goldie; Hector McKinnon; Tommy Gillan. *Front row:* Jimmy McConnochie; Jack Gilmour; Fraser McIntosh; Jimmy Laird; Robert Barr. Amateur teams from the mainland play for the Finlayson Cup throughout the summer annually. The cup is named after the late Jimmy Finlayson, a local man and sports officer in the 1st Millport Boys Brigade.

The puffer *Spartan*, photographed in July 1968, was the last boat to use the Tottie Pier. She was delivering pipes for use in the drainage system at the new coup at White Bay. The Tottie Pier got its name as it was from here that potatoes were transported from Millport farms to the mainland. It was only accessible at high tide.

The *Marchioness of Graham*, en route from Millport to Arran, photographed at Keppel Pier. This pier was situated on the east side of the island almost opposite Fairlie. The house at the top of the pier was where the piermaster lived and the building to its left was a shop which sold mostly confectionery and ice cream. Public toilets stood next to it. Boats called at both the Old and Keppel Piers en route to the mainland, and Police Sergeant Cassels was known to buy a ticket from one to the other at a cost of 6*d*. He then walked back through the town to his house at the police station in order to do his rounds. The *Marchioness of Graham* was launched in 1936 and made her first public sailing in June of that year. During the war years she maintained the Wemyss Bay/Millport service. From 1946 she was on the Fairlie/Millport/Arran service in winter and continued various Clyde sailings until 1957. She was sold in 1958 for service in Greek waters and was laid up at Piraeus in 1968 and broken up a few years later.

Taken in 1984, this photograph shows the building of the new pier for the marine biological station next to Keppel Pier. The original pier was demolished at the same time as its replacement was built, but the former piermaster's house still stands and is now owned by the marine station. There has been a marine research station at Millport since 1885 when an old lighter was brought from Granton and anchored at Port Loy, a sheltered cove at Marine Parade. Called the *Ark*, this was used as a laboratory and marine research was carried out on it until it foundered in a very bad storm in 1900. In 1897 a permanent building was erected opposite Keppel Pier and students and professors from the UK and abroad came to work there. It became part of the Scottish Marine Biological Association in 1914, and a large new building was added beside the original one in 1939.

In 1970 the station ceased to be part of the Scottish Marine Biological Association but research continued from the same site under the direction of London and Glasgow Universities. Now called the University Marine Biological Station, it still flourishes and many student classes come to work and live temporarily in a hostel beside the original buildings. The station has two research vessels: the *Aplysia* for inshore work and a larger boat called the *Aora*. As Chancellor of the University of London, Princess Anne paid a visit to the marine biological station in 1995. This photograph shows Mr Bobby Wilkie speaking to the Princess, Professor John Davenport and Lord Lt. Major Henderson.

The Millport puffer *Saxon* is seen here at her usual berth in the harbour. She was owned by Walter Kerr (known as Saxon Kerr after his boat as there were two other local men with the same name). *Saxon* brought coal – generally from Ardrossan or Troon – for local merchants and also the gasworks, along with lime and other supplies for farmers and builders. She was also once used in the making of the Para Handy TV series. Built in 1920 with a steam engine powered by coal, she could carry 90 to 100 tons of cargo. Her length was 71' 9" and her breadth 18' 3". After Walter Kerr retired in 1966 *Saxon* was broken up.

This photograph was taken in 1974 and shows the yacht *White Heather* which had just arrived from the USA. It was owned by James B. Kerr, youngest son of ex-Provost Walter Kerr. Jim had sailed the yacht across the Atlantic from America into his home town, along with one crew member. Jim was my brother and when I was writing a story about the *White Heather* for the local paper I asked him the surname of this young man. He said he didn't know, as there was no need! After about two years at home, Jim sailed back to the States on his own.

This building at the Old Pier contained the piermaster's office, booking office, waiting room and toilets. After this photograph was taken *c*.1960 a second storey was added, although the building is no longer in use today. Here, a suitcase can be seen outside the booking office. Having purchased their tickets, travellers paid 4*d*. to go through the turnstiles and down the pier to the boat. Clyde passenger steamers called at the Old Pier until 1972, at which point modern passenger ferries using Cumbrae Slip were introduced.

The turnstiles at the Old Pier where pier dues were collected. It cost fourpence to go down the pier, whether or not you were travelling on the boats. Season ticket holders and contractors who had special licenses used the gate at the side. The clock was donated to the town by Provost Cockburn, who held office from 1907 to 1909. When the turnstiles were demolished in 1962 the clock was placed on top of the weighbridge building. It was replaced by a similar clock in 1975.

The Old Pier in its heyday with a puffer and one of the ferry boats – either the *Ashton* or the *Leven* – at its stern. There is also a passenger boat at the other side of the pier. The turnstile building can be seen with the clock on top. It is of interest to note that on 25 May 1968 there were 34 arrivals and departures from this pier, an unusually large number. The Royal George Hotel, on the right, is one of Cumbrae's oldest hotels and is still in business. Millport has two bus companies operating services from the Old Pier to the ferry slip, running in conjunction with the ferry timetable. Millport Motors has been owned by the Morrison family for three generations. The other company, Cumbrae Coaches, is run by Sandy Wright. During the summer months a Stagecoach open top bus does tours round the island with appropriate commentary.

WAY IN
PENCE

The Old Pier after a storm. The white building
at its end was the signal box. This had three
round windows and by pushing slides up the
piermaster could change the colour of the windows from
white to black, thereby indicating to skippers on which side
he wanted them to bring their vessels. The shed to the signal
box's left was used to store goods brought in by passenger boats
until the pier lorry came to collect them. Decking on the pier was not
nailed down so in the event of a storm it rose up and floated off. As
the only wind which really affects Millport comes from the south-
west the decking ended up on the beach. The planks were numbered
so it was quite easy to reassemble them; had the decking been fixed
down, large storm waves washing underneath the pier would have
lifted the piles out of the sea bed, thus causing major damage. In the
left foreground is the pier lorry which was bringing planks back to be
replaced. The man on the lorry is Joe Morgan.

Millport had what was believed to be the first public hovercraft service in the world, introduced in 1965 and running between the town and Largs. It departed from the beach at Kames Bay and arrived at Largs on the slipway near Aubrey Crescent (this had been built for flying boats during the war). The crossing took about eight minutes, depending on the weather. This photograph, taken in June 1970, shows the hovercraft arriving at Kames Bay. The fare was £1 for a single journey, making it substantially more expensive than the steamer service.

A 1965 photograph showing people waiting to board the hovercraft. Others have gathered just to have a look. After the passengers were on board and the engine started, the hovercraft rose up on its apron and shot off down the beach. I once asked what it was registered as and was shown a certificate on which it was classed as an aircraft. The hovercraft service was withdrawn c.1971.

This building was built during the Second World War for the Navy and was known locally as the Hush Hush because of its mysterious purpose. It is believed to have been used as an anti-submarine detection radar station. After the war it was used for various projects but gradually fell into a state of disrepair. In 1992, on one of her TV challenges, Anneka Rice helped upgrade the building. It is now called the Greycraigs Outdoor Centre and is run by St George's and St Peter's Church, Easterhouse as a holiday home for children.

When Anneka Rice finished her TV challenge to refurbish the Hush Hush at the north of the island, she asked 200 cyclists to cycle from the Old Pier to the opening ceremony. They are seen here assembling at the pier.

Demolition of the local gasworks in 1983. These were built in the 1840s by a small private company and situated behind Barend Street at the east end of Millport. They were acquired by the town council in 1896 and nationalised in 1949. The works produced coal gas, which was made by baking coal to drive off the volatile gas contained in it; this was then stored and distributed for lighting etc. Once the coal had had gas extracted from it, the residue, called coke, could be sold as a by-product. There were two gas holders next to the gasworks.

This building was Cumbrae's slaughterhouse, situated behind Penmachrie Farm. After its closure in 1940 an incinerator was installed there in the early 1950s and the large chimney in the picture was built. It is no longer in use as rubbish from the island is now taken to the mainland by refuse lorry rather than burnt locally. There is no longer a slaughterhouse on Cumbrae. The island has six farms: Breakough; Ballikillet; Portrye; Mid Kirkton; Figgitoch; and Ballochmartin. With the exception of the latter, which has a dairy herd, these are stock and arable farms. (Penmachrie is no longer a farm, but Ronnie Stewart lives there and runs his business, Cumbrae Carriers, from there.) Cumbrae's farmers, who were previously tenants of Lord Bute, were able to buy their lands and homes in 2000.

This building, which was situated at 60 Howard Street at the corner of Reid Street, was known locally as the Bute Hall. It was built in 1864 as a church with a gallery for the United Presbyterian Church, and when the congregation moved elsewhere it was bought by George Hastie, painter, and used as his office and workshop. Over the years it was owned by three generations of his family. Prior to the First World War a special floor was laid and for a short time it was used as a roller skating rink. During the Second World War when the local school had many evacuees on its roll and there was insufficient room to accommodate them, the gallery area was made into a schoolroom. When numbers dwindled again the hall became vacant, and afterwards the library was housed there for a short time. The building gradually deteriorated. After some time it was demolished and a house has now been built on the site.

Two old houses at the junction of Cardiff Street and Crawford Street being demolished in 1962. During this operation many bottles were found in the eaves of the buildings. It was thought these had been used by smugglers, and evidently brandy was one of the things that they brought in.

The actor Duncan Macrae had a home in Millport where he spent much of his spare time. In 1963 he took the lead role in a short film shot on the island for the Andy Stewart Spectacular Show. In it he played the part of a land worker who saves up to go to London. This picture, taken at Ballikillet road end on the Ferry Road, shows him talking to a number of local children who had volunteered to be extras.

Cumbrae School class of 1958.

Back row: Mrs Gunn; Frank Logan; Fleming Smith; Hunter Blair; Tom Barbour; James Hill; Alan Sinclair; Terence Kerr; Jimmy Fraser; Walter Chalmers; Robert McDowall; Mrs Rae. *Third row:* William McIntyre; David Johnstone; Wallace Pearce; Bill Burns; Colin Miller; John Shearer; David Stevenson; Gordon Gourley; Bill Lynch; Edward Doig. *Second row:* Moira Martin; Brenda Smith; Sandra Finlayson; Maureen Hunter; Mary Clark; Jean Burns; Margaret Pearce; Margaret Watt; Christine Mortimer; Alison McDermid; Marie Caval. *Front row:* Christopher Holton; Robin Sinclair; John Burns; Guido De Angelis; Derek Clark; Jimmy Hill; David Hutchison; Gordon Smith; Jim Peacock; Ken Cameron.

At present Cumbrae Primary School has 75 pupils, with 12 in the nursery class. Pupils travel daily to Largs Academy for secondary education.

Flooding is not really a problem on Cumbrae – the geography of the island means that rainwater just runs to the sea. But during the winter of 1975/76 the burn which runs down to Kames Bay became choked and caused flooding in the fields behind the housing scheme.

In 1968 there had been a long dry spell and a very hot summer, with the result that Millport ran out of gravitation water. Many of the larger houses had old wells in their gardens which were opened up and put in use; elsewhere drilling rigs such as the one pictured here were brought in. Water was found at various points and Millport survived the drought. Some of the locals were hoping that oil would be found!

The two reservoirs situated at the golf course ran dry during the drought of 1968; this picture shows the lower one. As the outlet pipes were fractionally higher than the bottom, pumps were used to extract the last of the water. All of Millport's water is now pumped from the mainland and the two reservoirs are used by the local angling club.

This 1954 photograph is unusual as Millport very rarely gets snow. The housing scheme is not nearly as big as it is at the present day and some houses have yet to be built in Ferry Road. The fire station was built in 1973 and now forms part of this panorama. Cumbrae's fire brigade consists of fourteen personnel and there is one fire engine and one tender – in the event of a large fire extra appliances are brought over from the mainland. Health services on the island are provided by a husband and wife team of doctors supported by a locum when necessary. There is a fourteen bed hospital half a mile from Millport for short-stay patients. When further investigation is required patients are transferred by ambulance via the ferry to either Inverclyde Hospital at Greenock or Crosshouse at Kilmarnock. Outwith ferry hours an air ambulance helicopter lands at the public park at West Bay. The island has two resident police constables.

The end of Guildford Street next to the Garrison c.1960. The shop on the far left was McLachlan's fish shop. The next shop with the white notice in the window was the burgh office before it became a hairdresser's belonging first to Tommy Counsell and then Isobel Anderson; at present it is owned by Colin Miller. Next along was the co-operative, now the VG store. The last two shops are still the same – Macfarlane's butcher owned by David Cameron and the post office.

Wallace's grocers shop stood at the foot of Cardiff Street and had one window in Cardiff Street and another facing the square at Quayhead. It was owned by the Wallace family of Millport for at least three generations. The last member of the family to run the shop was Ann, who took over the business when her father Matt died. She eventually sold it and it became the Nixe snack bar; at present is the Minstrel Wine Bar. Pictured is Ann (right) and her shop assistant Deena Boll.

The Nixe snack bar photographed *c*.1957 shortly after it opened. It was owned by Andrew Dick, who had a tearoom in the Garrison, and his son Andy who had a snack bar at the rear of the Garrison. After opening the Nixe, Mr Dick and family moved out of the Garrison altogether.

Dan Millar, still wearing his cycle clips having just arrived back at his shop after delivering an order. Next to him is his wife (centre) and their assistant Mrs G. MacDonald. The photograph was taken outside their licensed grocer's shop at 9 Kelburn Street in 1956. The shop is still there but under new management.

Mr & Mrs Hector McKinnon's fruit and vegetable shop at 3 Glasgow Street photographed in 1958. Hector retired in the early 1980s and the shop is now a florists under different management. The photograph shows Hector with his sisters and mother. From left to right they are: Elizabeth (known as Toosh), Mrs McKinnon, Hector, Flora and Margaret.

Miss Morton at the door of her shop, the last remaining shop in Stuart Street. After she retired it became a shoe shop owned by Mrs Mathieson. It is currently an ice cream parlour.

Part of Guildford Street photographed in the early 1960s. The shop that can just be seen on the extreme left was McKay, grocer; next to it is Mapes cycle and toy shop, then McDougall's shoe shop followed by Hastie's confectioners. The small window to the right of Hastie's belonged to Kerr's photographic studio, with the photographer's fancy goods shop next door. In the foreground is part of the crazy golf course. The lady in the centre with the brush is Mrs Hill, who was in charge of the crazy golf and lived across the road at 10 Guildford Street.

Staff at Millport post office. The photograph was taken for Mrs Guthrie and shows her, her family and postal workers prior to her retirement in 1956. *Left to right:* Archie Guthrie; Jessie Guthrie (married name McDowall); Aimee Guthrie (married name Elliott); Mrs Guthrie (postmistress); David Finlayson; Duncan Cassells; George Brown. The latter three were all postmen.

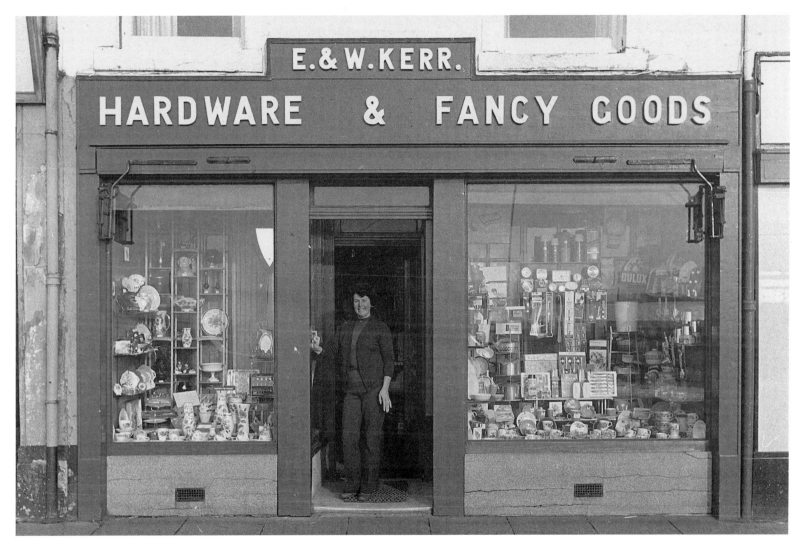

The shop owned by Euphemia and Walter Kerr at 23 Stuart Street has now been converted into a house. Before Walter and Effie bought the business it belonged to sisters Jenny and Mary Kerr, cousins of Walter's father. Prior to that it had been a drapers shop. Effie is seen at the door of the shop.

Donkey and pony rides on Millport Beach have always been popular. In this 1961 picture, Gillian Miller is standing between the two ponies and the girl at the donkey and trap is her sister Lesley. They are the daughters of the late Tom and Frances Miller who were teachers at Millport school for some time. Both girls are now married and each have families of their own. The horses, ponies and donkeys were originally owned by the Macdonald family and were stabled in College Street, adjacent to the Cathedral of the Isles. The present owner is Mrs Christine McCulloch and the stables are at Upper Kirkton, on the Golf Road. During the summer the ponies and donkeys are still to be seen on the beach.

In the days when rowing boats were hired out to the public there were two Millport boat-hirers at the Strathwherry jetty – Alex Hunter and James Mauchline. As well as the communal stone jetty, they each had a private jetty (obscured behind the notice boards in this photograph). These jetties were used for their motor boats which made trips to Largs, Kilchattan Bay and the Wee Cumbrae. James Mauchline built his own boats which were all named *Triumph*. The last one is thought to have been *Triumph IV*. Alex Hunter also built some of his boats and one was named *Sunbeam*. He also had a large cabin cruiser called *Cramond Brig* which he bought in 1934. Hunter's boat shed was at the right hand side of the jetty while Mauchline's (not visible in this picture) was to the left of the slipway.

The BBC's Children's Caravan programme was broadcast live outside Downcraig Cottage at the site of the old ferry pier in June 1960. A large marquee was erected and a show was performed in front of an audience of local children. One of the artists appearing in the variety show was Cardew 'The Cad' Robinson.